DELARA & NOWRUZ

words & design by
Minoo B.
illustrations by
Azadeh S.

DELARA WAKES UP EVERY MORNING
EARLIER THAN THE SUN.

SHE RUSHES TO HER MOM AND
SHAKES HER LIKE IT'S FUN.

"MAMAN! MAMAN! ARE YOU AWAKE?"

HER MOM ALWAYS HAS A SMILE.

IF YOU KNOW HER,
YOU KNOW THAT'S HER USUAL STYLE.

"OH, HONEY, THE CLOCK SAYS IT'S ONLY SIX. YOU
CAN COME AND SNUGGLE FOR A FEW MORE TICKS."

MOM OPENED HER EYES, HER VOICE STILL LOW.

SHE SAID, "YOU KNOW WHAT? LET'S GET
DOWN AND START THE SABZEH TO GROW.

WE CAN SOAK THE WHEAT IN A BOWL,
AT LEAST.

LIKE WE ALWAYS DO EVERY YEAR FOR THE
NOWRUZ FEAST."

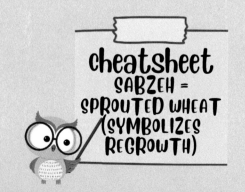

cheatsheet
SABZEH =
SPROUTED WHEAT
(SYMBOLIZES
REGROWTH)

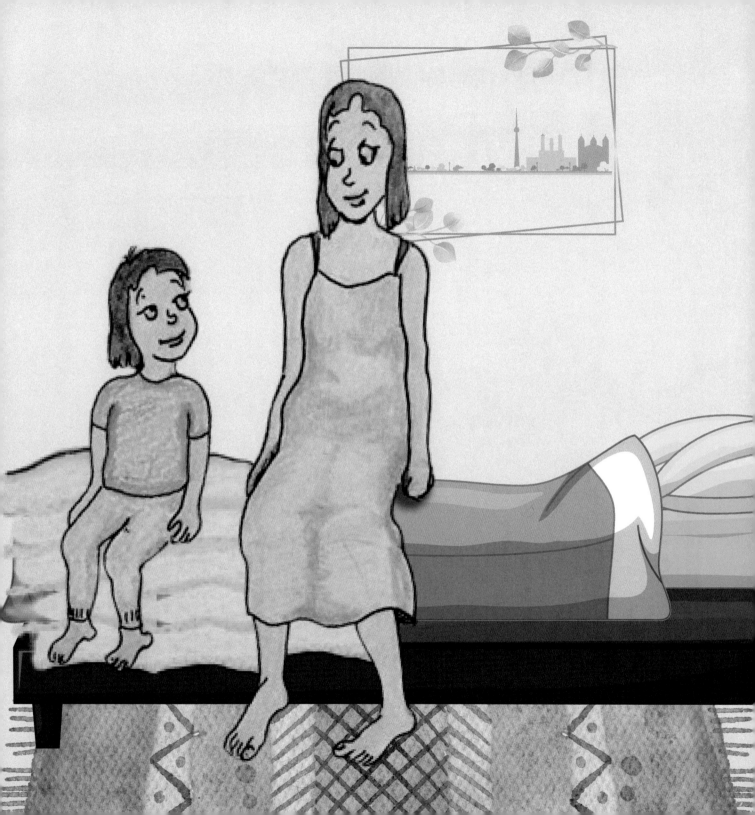

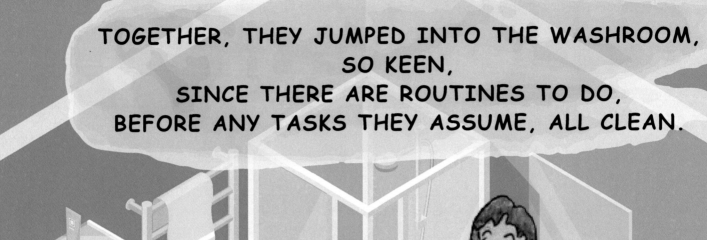

TOGETHER, THEY JUMPED INTO THE WASHROOM,
SO KEEN,
SINCE THERE ARE ROUTINES TO DO,
BEFORE ANY TASKS THEY ASSUME, ALL CLEAN.

MOM SAID,
"REMEMBER OUR SPECIAL WAY;

WE ADD THE WHEAT LITTLE BY LITTLE,
CALLING THE ROLL

NAMING ALL LOVED ONES WHILE PUTTING
THE WHEAT IN THE BOWL.

WE NAME MAMANI, BABAYI,
AUNTS, UNCLES IN OUR CALL..."

DELARA GOT EXCITED AND YELLED:
"MY FRIENDS JAMIE, GLORIA, SHELLY & HA JOON,
CAUSE THEY'RE, TOO, MY ALL!"

MOM CONTINUED,
"JAMIE, GLORIA, SHELLY, HA JOON,
AND ALL THE COUSINS..."

SHE LOOKED AT DELARA,
AND HER PRIDE GREW BY DOZENS.

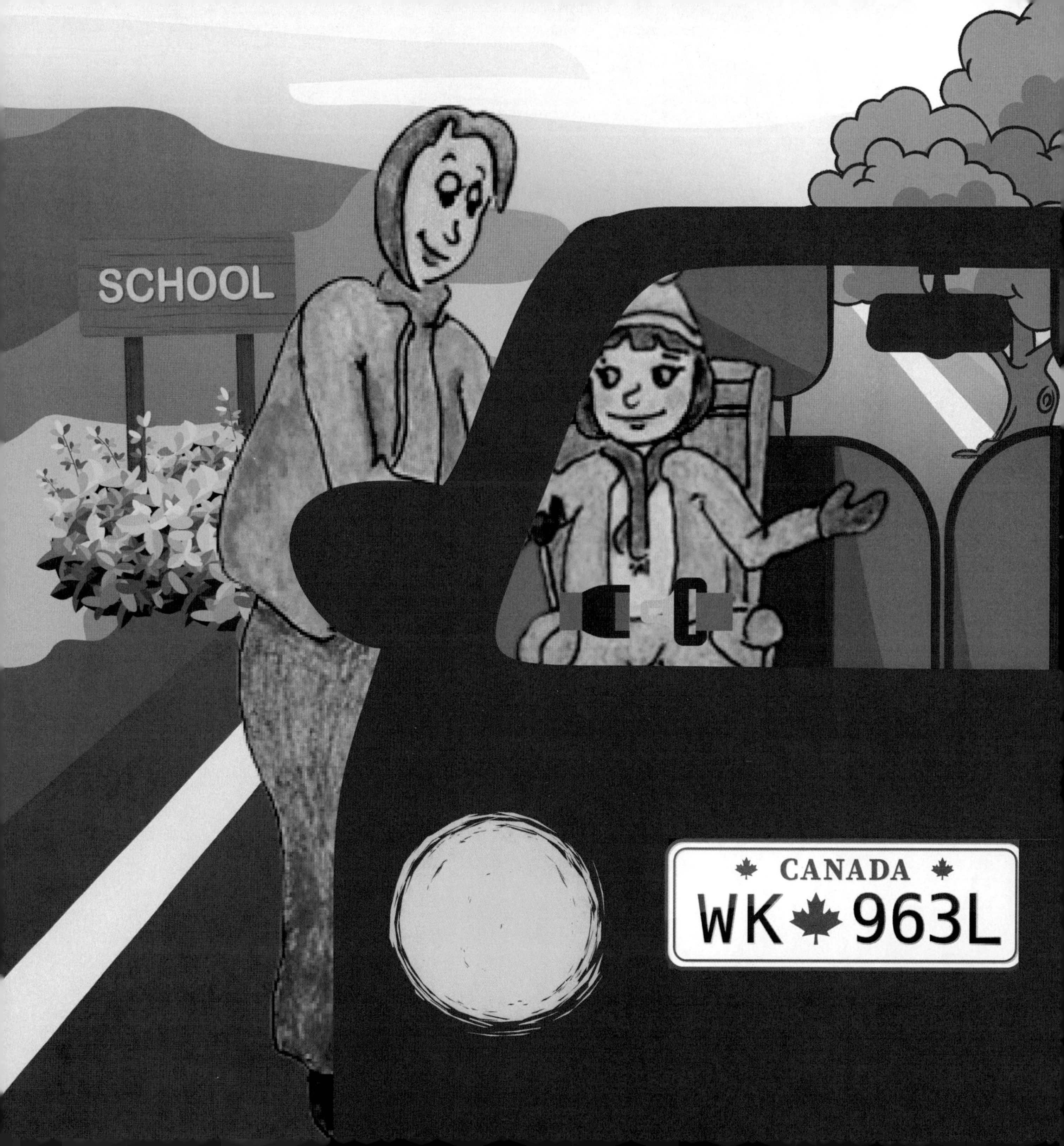
SCHOOL
CANADA
WK 963L

LATER IN THE CAR, AS SCHOOL CAME INTO VIEW,
MOM SAID TO DELARA, "GO AHEAD TO YOUR CREW,
SHARE WHAT HAPPENED AND ALL THAT WAS DONE,
ABOUT NOWRUZ PREPARATIONS AND ALL THE FUN."

DELARA WENT TO SCHOOL ALL HAPPY AND MERRY,
SINCE THE NEW YEAR WAS COMING WITH ALL ITS
MAGIC AND GLORY.

DELARA GATHERED HER FRIENDS AROUND,
SO EXCITED.
AND TALKED ABOUT SABZEH AND ALL,
SUPER DELIGHTED.

BUT THEN, JAMIE WENT, "HAH?!..."
"HA JOON SAID, " WHAT??"

SHELLY WAS JUST STARING.

AND JAMIE WAS SLURRING:
"SEZZE.. SZZZZZ...? WHAT DID I JUST HEAR?"

DELARA INSISTED, "IT'S NOWRUZ,
THE NEW YEAR;
WHAT IS NOT CLEAR?"

JAMIE SAID, "BUT DEL! NEW YEAR'S HAS
JUST GONE!
LET'S STOP KIDDING AND GO AND HAVE
SOME FUN!"

SHE TRIED TO SPEAK BUT MERELY GROANED.
NOBODY KNEW NOWRUZ! SHE FELT SO ALONE.

ON THE RIDE BACK, MOM PEERED
IN THE MIRROR WITH CARE,

KNOWING WELL WHAT LAY
IN DEL'S HEART, DEEPLY HIDDEN THERE.

GENTLY, MOM ASKED,
"DID SOMETHING TODAY GIVE YOU PAIN?"

DELARA REPLIED,
"THEY DON'T KNOW NOWRUZ; MY JOY'S IN VAIN!"

"OH, DEAR ONE, NOWRUZ IS OURS TO HOLD,
IT'S TRUE,
BUT PERHAPS THERE'S A WAY
TO SHARE IT ANEW.
HOW MIGHT YOU INVOLVE THEM,
WHAT CAN YOU CONVEY?
TOGETHER,
LET'S THINK OF A WAY
TO BRIGHTEN THEIR DAY."

AT SUPPER, MOM SAID, "YOU KNOW DEL,
SAAL TAHVIL IS ON THE WEEKEND THIS YEAR;
PERFECT TIMING, HUH?"
DELARA JUMPED IN THE AIR, YELLING,
"I GOT IT, MOM!"

"I CAN INVITE THEM OVER; WHAT DO YOU THINK?
WITH THEM WE WILL SHARE OUR HAFT-SEEN!"
HER MOOD CHANGED IN A BLINK!

"OH, DEAR! THAT'S GREAT. I'M SO PROUD.
WE ALWAYS LOVE TO CELEBRATE LOUD
WITH A CROWD!"

DELARA KEPT TALKING.
HER IDEAS WERE FLOWING:

"WE SAVE SOME EGGS TO COLOUR TOGETHER.
MY FRIENDS AND I LOVE PAINTING FOREVER AND EVER."

"SOUNDS GREAT, HONEY!
HOW ABOUT AN INVITE?
SHOULD WE MAKE SOME,
JUST TO BE POLITE?"

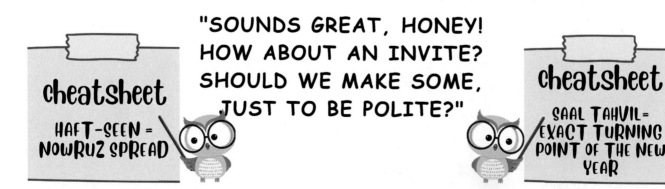

cheatsheet

HAFT-SEEN =
NOWRUZ SPREAD

cheatsheet

SAAL TAHVIL=
EXACT TURNING
POINT OF THE NEW
YEAR

DELARA AND MOM STARTED
CUTTING AND DRAWING,
MAKING INVITES
WHILE IDEAS WERE POPPING.

THEY THOUGHT IT WOULD BE FUN
TO ASK EACH FRIEND, IF THEY WANT,
TO BRING AN ITEM FROM THE HAFT-SEEN
TO FEEL BELONGED.

ON THE INVITES, THEY DREW
APPLE, GARLIC, CANDLE, COIN
FOR THE FRIENDS AND PARENTS
TO PREPARE BEFORE THEY JOIN.

DELARA THOUGHT THE CARDS
TURNED OUT GREAT.
SHE WAS EXCITED FOR TOMORROW,
SHE REALLY COULDN'T WAIT.

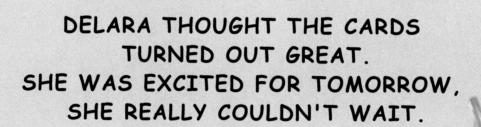

LET'S CELEBRAT
TOGETHER AT MY
YOUR PARENTS A
THAN WELCOME T

PLS RSVP BY MARC
P.S.: IF YOU WANT, YOU C
A CANDLE
TO PUT ON OUR NOWRUZ
CALLED "SOFREH HAFT-

BA BOUSEH,
DELARA

LET'S CELEBRA
TOGETHER AT
YOUR PARENT
THAN WELCO

PLS RSVP BY
P.S.: IF YOU WA
SOME GARLIC
TO PUT ON OUR
CALLED "SOF

BA BOUS
DELARA

YOU'RE INVITED!
LET'S CELEBRATE NOWRUZ
TOGETHER AT MY PLACE.
YOUR PARENTS ARE MORE
THAN WELCOME TO JOIN US!

PLS RSVP BY MARCH 15TH.
P.S.: IF YOU WANT, YOU CAN BRING
A RED APPLE
TO PUT ON OUR NOWRUZ SPREAD,
CALLED "SOFREH HAFT-SEEN".

BA BOUSEH,
DELARA

cheatsheet

BA BOUSEH =
KISSES

THE NEXT DAY, DELARA WENT TO SCHOOL WITH
THE INVITES IN HER HANDS,

SHE KNEW THAT BY TALKING ABOUT NOWRUZ THIS
TIME, THEY ALL WOULD UNDERSTAND.

SHE JUMPED IN ALL EXCITED AND SAID:
"LET'S GATHER FOR LOTS OF NOWRUZ FUN
TO SPREAD."

JAMIE, GLORIA, SHELLY & HA JOON
THEY JUMPED AND WENT OVER THE MOON.

ON THE DAY OF SAAL TAHVIL,
THE TIME HAD COME AT LAST,
TO SET THE HAFT-SEEN,
A LINK TO THEIR PAST.

WITH SONBOL, SENJED,
AND SAMANU, THE PERSIAN DELIGHT,
SOMAGH, SIB, AND SEER,
A BEAUTIFUL SIGHT.

SONBOL
HYACINTHUS

SERKEH
VINEGAR

SABZEH
SPROUT

SA'AT
CLOCK

SIB
APPLE

SENJED
A DATE

SEKKEH ADDED LAST,
SHINING LIKE THE SUN,
SEVEN 'S' ITEMS,
THEIR NOWRUZ HAD BEGUN.

GUESTS CAME OVER AND WERE WELCOMED
WITH TEA, PASTRY, AND CANTALOUPE.

CELEBRATING TOGETHER,
THEIR JOY IS AS VAST AS THE GLOBE.

THEY INSTANTLY FELT CLOSE,
A WARM ATMOSPHERE THEY DID STIR,
"SUCH A RICH BLEND OF FOOD AND CULTURE,"
THEY THOUGHT, FEELING THE ALLURE.

MOM JOINED THE KIDS,
GATHERED AT THE TABLE'S SIDE,

LAUGHING AND PAINTING EGGS,
WITH JOY THEY COULDN'T HIDE.

THE DAY CAME TO AN END,
THEY WERE ALL HUGGING LIKE A GREAT FRIEND.

HA JOON'S MOM CAME CLOSE,
SAYING ALL GOOD THINGS ABOUT NOWRUZ
WITH A BEAUTIFUL POSE.

SHE HAD A GREAT SUGGESTION
"LET'S ALL CELEBRATE CHUSEOK AT OUR PLACE,
NEXT THANKSGIVING DAY, PLEASE MAKE SOME SPACE."

DELARA'S MOM WAS SO DELIGHTED,
WHAT BETTER ENDING COULD BE FORESIGHTED?

cheatsheet
CHUSEOK =
KOREAN
THANKSGIVING DAY

IN DELARA'S COZY ROOM,
AS NIGHT GENTLY FELL,
MOM LAY BESIDE HER,
A STORY TO TELL.

"TODAY WAS SO LOVELY,
FROM START TO END,
ABOUT A THOUGHTFUL GIRL,
WHO'S A WONDERFUL FRIEND.

SHE FELT A BIT SAD,
HER CULTURE UNKNOWN,
BUT INSTEAD OF SORROW,
A BRIGHT IDEA WAS BORN.

SHE SHARED HER NOWRUZ,
WITH FRIENDS SO DEAR,
CREATING A CIRCLE OF FRIENDSHIP,
FILLED WITH CHEER.

THIS GIRL, SO CREATIVE,
WITH A HEART SO GRAND,
BROUGHT HER WORLD TO OTHERS,
HELPING THEM UNDERSTAND.
NOW CLOSE YOUR EYES, MY DEAR,
AND DRIFT TO DREAMS SO SWEET,
OF DAYS FILLED WITH SHARING,
MAKING EVERY MOMENT A TREAT."

WITH THESE GENTLE WORDS,
DELARA'S EYES CLOSED TIGHT,
DREAMING OF CULTURES SHARED,
IN THE SOFT MOONLIGHT.

Made in the USA
Las Vegas, NV
12 March 2024

87089776R00021